CONTENTS

1.	All is well in the world or is it?	4
2.	Old dog new tricks	15
3.	That first networking event	19
4.	Done first event now what?	24
5.	Job club revisited	29
6.	Networking groups	33
7.	Reintroduction to LinkedIn	38
8.	Networking is good but	42
9.	Review and move forward	48
10.	Acronyms and clichés	52
11.	Do your market research	60
12.	Blogs	64
13.	Tips	83
14.	Keep on track	92
15.	The Networking Conversion System	98

CHAPTER ONE

All is well with the world, or is it?

Networking
It's all about the room

Foreword

The reason I have written this book and the follow up, is that I wanted to give back to a world that helped me when I needed it most.

From being made redundant to where I am now and will be in the future is mainly down to those people I have met along the way.

These books cover my journey with all its highs and lows, but mainly the massive positive experience of Networking and LinkedIn.

Within these pages I will recall that journey and with it the people I met and more importantly the things that I learned from them. Most of the advice and knowledge came free, but I did spend some money on training as well. That was a large investment from someone who was in my position, but the biggest investment was my time. Time that I spent building those relationship to the point where they are today and all the benefits they bring.

My philosophy for my business and in writing this book is to HELP, I want to give people access to what I have learned over the past decade so they can make informed choices and not make the mistakes I made. I want to make people aware of the good and bad points of networking, so people who find themselves on their own journeys can benefit from my experience and shorten the time it takes to be effective.

I hope that you enjoy my journey but my real aim with these books is to demonstrate the power of both Networking and LinkedIn to people in business or looking to start a business, because good relationships are invaluable in work and life.

Hello and welcome to my world, well the last 10 years of it mainly, a world of downs and ups. During this period, I went through many changes in circumstances and learnt many things which I think will help people who find themselves in similar and parallel positions.

During this period, I went from being a stable if unspectacular member of staff to where I am now, self-employed and helping others. I have had to learn new skills and realise that you need to break out of your comfort zone to truly become the person you can be.
I coined a phrase a few years back which I still use regularly. It was "I was in a "Velvet Groove". I believe a lot of people reside there and never really get out of it. The reason for this is in the title, in a "velvet" grove. This refers to when you find yourself in a comfortable and not to taxing a position. Let's face it we put up with a lot of shit jobs and shit employers because the actual role we do does not tax us greatly. Stress us yes, but that is self-inflicted!! (more on that soon), but it is all a bit too comfortable and we can convince ourselves that it is ok. No, it is not ok to not fulfil your promise, to do what you deserve to do, you need to get out of that "Velvet Groove", but it's convenient, and so the argument goes on within your head.

I know this is not just me and after having had a chat with a few colleagues, they have confirmed this to me. Pointing this out to a few of them motivated them to get out of the grove take a risk, and to move on somewhere new. Yes, I am good at managing others' lives, people were often coming to me for advice as they knew I would have an opinion, but also, I would not sugar coat.

That was great, and I loved helping but it was not helping me help myself. It is always easier to settle for what you have got, but if you have even thought about leaving when you are in a reflective mood, not just after one of those days, then that is enough doubt to make you think seriously. Do a snap shot of where you are in life versus where you would like to be or even better where you are on your way to your goal.

There are enough books on goals, but even after a degree of cynicism myself in this goal setting, I found they are actually very powerful, especially if chunked into small manageable parts. If you are where you want to be then great, this book is of no use to you at all, use it for that wobbly table leg. But, if you start to see some contradictions between where you are and where you want to be, coming into play then you need to look much deeper.

An example from my history is that I had a role that did not pay well, for a company where I could have done a lot more for them, but it was under 2 miles from home. Yes, a reasonable work life balance could be had and that was my plus side for being in my "velvet groove". For other's it will be the hassle involved with looking for a new job, and yes, I can truly understand that, and it will be easier just to stay and put up with it. People will also think it is not always greener on the other side, or better the devil you know. Well here is where I refer to the stress element that you regularly find yourself in when you are in a job that is really a bad fit with your ambition. The main culprit of this stress is you. If you are in a job you don't enjoy, that does not push you, then you will stress yourself about it because you know you are better than this. It is even worse when colleagues tell you this believe me.

It is nice that they see your potential even if the bosses can't, but you can only really blame yourself. You are after all the one who has decided to let this situation continue. For me it would have been better if the job was miles away and commuting cut into my day, giving me more reason to move on. I have not even mentioned money and I am ashamed to say the role that was 2 miles away also payed me around 60% of what I had been earning!!

So, this book is here to help teach you some tools to escape this situation, as well as also being aimed at people who are at this point for other reasons. Some will get here through no choice of their own others will choose to go on this route of breaking free from the role that is drowning their ambition.

What they all have in common with each other and in common with me 9 years ago, is they are not truly ready to go on this route. We may want to leave the role or have been made redundant, or you want to go it alone. Regardless of how you find yourself at this position of preparing to take on the business world alone or even with a partner, it is a fact that there are few people or courses that truly teaches you what to do. lots of people give general advice but the people I meet and the ones this book is aimed at are not given enough of the right advice or training to start out. As I have stated some will, like me, find themselves jobless, but not by choice, others will choose to stop working for others and want to go it alone, and there are many shades in-between. Add in other factors such as in my case, my age, then things stack up against you. What I am trying to do with this book and the associated products is to help people through this tricky period and hopefully get to where they want to go.

What makes me qualified to write this as my first book is that I have not only been there I have seen many others at various stages in need of help. Along the way I have met some wonderful people who have been willing to help, and I make no apologies for mentioning them throughout the book. These are the people who I went to for help or they came to me to offer it. Most of them have got where they are by really demanding work, going through tough times and bouncing back.

They have become leaders within their fields and I am proud to say that I know them and that they have helped me and many others. Some are internationally known, easily earning 6 figure incomes, but still respect and help others who know how to approach them.

As well as all my hero's there are all those that I have tried to help myself, albeit from the position of an employed person, with advice and signposting. They have been a mixture of new start-ups, people in year 1 and struggling, people coming into owner managed from corporate world (often with a nice pay-out) as well as the unemployed.

My journey has taken 9 years and what I want to do within this book is to try and shorten the time of your own journey. I intend to do this by letting you know all the mistakes I made and the time they cost me. Also, all the wonderful information I have come across and learned from my network. To add to this, I am also an avid reader of business and psychology books and will use what I have learnt there to help as well. I am also a Fellow of the Chartered Management Institute, and to be a fellow you must demonstrate at least 10 years in senior management.

So, to the story of how I came to be writing this book. I will use a lot of what I have learnt over this period and tell it in a story style as well as obvious hints and tips, the main ones I will highlight as we go through the book. I will also repeat some items and hints because this is based on real life and certain things just naturally re occur or I feel it is right to re enforce the information. I would rather be criticised for some repeats rather than for some omissions.

The Story starts back in 2008 and the recession had bitten hard. I am working in West London, in a job that I enjoy despite the elevated level of time related stress. The client list I had were all household names and wanted immediate responses. It Was Just another normal hectic day in the office when another, yet another email popped into my inbox. This time it was from the CEO wanting everyone to meet out on the factory floor in 15 minutes. I duly made my way along with my colleague's, all theorising on what it was about We got downstairs to add to the assembled masses and the hum of the assembled people talking. At the allotted time, he appeared before us. What happened over the next 3 hours was to affect my life in a big way. Even though there had been a round or redundancies around 6 months ago, the dark clouds had gathered again and there had to be more cuts.

We were called to the boardroom 1 by 1 to hear our fate, eventually it got to me (they did it alphabetically). It was explained to me that I was now under the threat of redundancy because of the big downturn in business. They explained what the process would be, but I must say little of it penetrated my consciousness, as redundancy was no stranger to me. It had been a fair few years since I faced this horribly destabilising situation.

At my next meeting, a few days later it was made clear that the downturn in my sector (Construction) was severe and that I could not be kept on along with 3 other account managers/directors. I was told that I could go home to let it sink in and that I could leave immediately if I wanted to. I chose neither and decided to take an early lunch and return to my desk after to continue work that afternoon.

I then had to make the hardest phone call of my life to my darling wife, to let her know my fate. I am not too proud to say that many tears were shed and not just by Stephanie. I returned to my desk as I had promised to do and tried to carry on with my work as best I could whilst listening to the redundancy rumours and speculations. Some of my colleagues had not taken it well and had left immediately, whilst others had stayed and disrupted the flow in the office. I could understand their feelings, but I thought it best to stay professional, and not to burn any bridges.

I had one further meeting, a 1-2-1 with the CEO whom I had first met when he was 18 as I supplied his company and knew his dad. His father had since passed away, but we had more of a connection than most, because of this. It was the most awkward 15 minutes you can imagine. Nothing much was said as I had accepted my fate and the reasons for it. You could see on his face the anguish of letting me go, having personally given me the key role in his company. It was made worse because he knew me previously and that his father had thought well of me.

My final day came for those of us that had chosen to work to the end. We went to the pub to say goodbye to those that had worked their months' notice. I had only let on I was one of the unlucky ones that morning, so there were some surprised faces. I left with my head held high knowing that I had been professional to the end. It felt weird leaving knowing that I would not be coming back the next working day, and the journey home was awash with emotions. I was greeted by my wife who gave me a large hug as she fought back the tears. That evening was solemn but the next morning was the weird one for me, as I crave security and I am highly organised, any like routine. I woke went downstairs and sat in my chair. I sat reflecting on the occurrences of the direct past and realised that I was now feeling alone in a world I did not understand. How was I to go about seeking work, how was I to survive on the pitiful dole money that I needed to claim. I had been an Account Director and was paid well, how was I to live day to day, my wife worked but, there was no way that we could survive on her wages alone. I needed to get to some money coming in, and fast.

After taking a few days to let it sink in I decided I needed to start looking for that new job. I decided to do what I had always done, send CV's to companies I knew in the industry, drop CV's around the local business estates and of course join as many job boards as I could find. The next thing was to sign up with as many suitable recruitment agencies as I could. I treated job hunting as a job in itself, and daily I sat at a computer looking for any opportunity as well as planning road trips to business centres. Well this is what I used to have to do earlier in my career, so it must be the right thing to do now, mustn't it?

> TREAT LOOKING FOR A JOB AS A JOB IN IT'S SELF

Well actually no, but at this stage I was not aware of that, and I got what I thought was a lucky break. I had got an interview via a contact at one of the largest companies I Account directed. So, I had done the right thing without even knowing it, I had built a relationship with this gentleman. So, when he found a new job, as he had lost his at the same time I had, he thought of me. He phoned my old boss and asked for my contact details. After a phone conversation, he put me forward for the position.

I had to do a presentation to a panel of three people and do an interview. I got the nod a few weeks later, and started soon after. I was reporting to my old contact and it all seemed very nice, as it was a charity and it felt good helping people. The downside was a charity salary was substantially less that I was used to.

Things went along fine for 14 months and I enjoyed managing the team and helping those in need. I had an office in the warehouse that was bigger than the floor space in my home!! The gentleman who got me the opportunity soon moved on as he could not cope with the lack of business acumen that the senior people had. I continued and was even running at a profit until an email popped into my inbox asking me to attend a meeting at Head Office that afternoon.... you can guess the rest, it was one of those meetings. Due to funding cuts I was let go and again cast back to that world that I was yet to get a handle on, over 50 and out of work

So, the cycle started again but with 1 momentous change this time. I had heard about Job Clubs, I can't remember where from, but this changed the whole job hunting landscape for me.

> ALWAYS LOOK FOR HELP, JOB CLUBS CAN GIVE INVALUABLE HELP

The Executive Job club was run by volunteers and held their meetings at alternate venues in my area. I remember my first one was at Windsor above the library. I entered the venue not knowing what to expect but determined I was going to participate and learn whatever I could. I was greeted with a smile and my particulars were taken down and then I was offered coffee, so a pleasant enough start. That first week was just about getting to know your fellow club members and the instructors who were all unpaid volunteers.

We were asked to make a diary of what we did from then until the next meeting, as we would be asked about it. The rest of the meeting was very relaxed, not at all stressful, in fact we were told it was alright to feel emotional, well for a week but no more. I left the meeting feeling a lot better about life and knowing that I had to make a plan. This was not an issue for me as I was an organised person and aware of SMART goals.

Looking back, I think that joining the group worked on so many levels for me. I was in a room with people who were also jobless, so I was not alone. It also made me accountable, especially to me, and I had a feeling of belonging, which being a sociable person ticked a very big box. I had people telling me what the market was like and how to go about looking for opportunities, which was invaluable.

> ALWAYS SET GOALS, BECAUSE WITHOUT THEM IT IS JUST HOPING

After that first meeting, I was committed to the 15-week programme, unless of course I was offered employment before the end (Positive Mental Attitude). The atmosphere was good, and the members were all executives, some having earnt substantially more than me, but more on that later, so we had some commonality there as well. It was a good fit and raised all our spirits, which was the exact opposite of having to sign on, which was a necessary evil for a few of us. Having to attend the Job Centre sucked hope away from you as the staff I met were very nice and friendly but ultimately clueless to my requirements. I entered the meeting room the next week with a folder stuffed with my activity and could not wait to show how committed I was and how serious I took this situation.

We all had an opportunity to tell our stories and it was obvious from what was said, that I was making the most effort. At the time, I put this down to my new-found optimism and being new to the club.

The third meeting was the one that changed everything. Having gone around the table asking us for our weekly updates, I was again praised for my efforts, but then as we had heard all members story the bombshell was dropped. Although my efforts had been praised, I and the others were told that it was mostly pointless and in fact a lot was a waste of time and resources!!!

> EFFORT IS GOOD BUT MAKE SURE IT IS NOT WASTED ON THE WRONG DISCIPLINES

We all sat down, our attention well and truly pricked and were told the truth of the current job market. This was that most advertised jobs were not real, recruitment agencies and online job boards just played a numbers game. The real jobs, which people of our level were looking for, were rarely advertised!

So how can you apply for a job that is not advertised?

We were told that we had to add 2 new disciplines to what we were doing. We were not to abandon the old ways completely as they might still work, and they satisfy the job centres requirements. Just don't waste too much time on them, we needed to put the effort into these 2 new activities. So, what were these 2 activities that now held the key to finding a new position?

We all sat around the long table and it was then explained to us that we needed to Network and use LinkedIn, there were some nods of recognition but generally blank looks.

We were told we all already networked but were probably unaware of it, and we now had to broaden what we had been doing and get proficient at it. Networking it turned out was attending any type of event and talking to people and telling them about yourself and your current situation!

The significant difference was now you needed to be very clear with your story, and that you had to take it to another level, you needed to fit into these new surroundings and treat it as if you were promoting something, it is just that this something was you.

So, we were advised to investigate going to business networking events and talking to people about the position we found ourselves in. They told us to look for these events and report back to the group. On my return to my home office I went straight onto my computer to search for these events.

After a very short period of searching it seemed that our area was rich with events at all times of day and at all levels. All we had to do was to find how to get invited to them or booked on, and then quite simply go along and start our network journey. Sounds simple enough, but how many of us is comfortable with talking to a load of strangers at the best of times. Then there is the added pressure of trying to sell the idea of you and your current position.

I suggest that not many will be truly comfortable with this notion, but the thought of having to do it regularly must actual scare some people. Most of the room had presented from time to time at various times of our working life. This though was very different, the pressure far greater, the rewards currently far higher than anything else before. We now all had to plan and refine our presentations, this networking seemed as if it could be quite brutal for some.

CHAPTER TWO

OLD DOG NEW TRICKS

To help us with this new presentation style we were introduced to the elevator pitch, so we could use it at any event, and on any other occasion that came along, which could be anywhere at any time!

This Elevator pitch seemed to be very important and something we need to get spot on. So, what is an elevator pitch and how would I use it? Well it transpires that an elevator pitch comes from the opportunity for someone to sell an idea to a decision maker.

The Elevator part is from America with all those ghastly high-rise office blocks. You would have to travel on the elevator on a regular basis to and from various departments, and you may find yourself in the elevator with a key decision maker. It is generally accepted that this gives you 1-2 minutes to put across your case before your captive audience gets out of the elevator. Some network groups teach this, and a lot give you the opportunity to stand up and deliver it, so It seemed important that you learnt how to work yours out and how to deliver it.

The Job club went about teaching us this skill and we practiced it each week, refining it and presenting it, with varying degrees of success. We were told, as with most things it gets better with practice.

Let's hope so

Now my opinion, and it is mine not a consensus, is that it does not work in its pure rehearsed form for many people. No two situations are exactly the same and therefore how can one rehearsed pitch work for all situations? You certainly need a framework when you engage with someone and have the opportunity to tell them your situation.

I have found that being very targeted on why you have engaged with the person is the key. There should be an outcome you have in mind, and this will change dependant on who you are speaking to and where you are at the time. You can see from this that a learned pitch will not sitwell with every occasion and you need to tailor it to the situation otherwise it could have completely the opposite effect. In fact, if it "salesy" in any way it most likely put off the other person. What you did need was a mental bullet point list to frame your pitch.

So, in my opinion, you need something between a rehearsed pitch and an off the cuff option, so that you can adapt to the situation. I would even suggest that you have one bullet point that you can mental call upon, that suggest that you meet up at a better time to discuss your idea.

They may be time poor at the time as well so you never know they just might say yes, what you don't want to do is walk away thinking "what have I achieved?"

Despite my misgivings now, I was back then, ready to accept any advice to help me with my situation, as I believe many will. So, as like the others in the group I crafted an elevator pitch and practiced it with the group. Some found it easier than others, some made them too rigid, others not professional enough. But practice we did to help improve the skill, some even managed to inject humour into it.

> ELEVATOR PITCHES CAN WORK AGAINST YOU SO DON'T MAKE THEM RIGID

So, where we were to go to put this skill to work and land yourself a nice new job? As I stated earlier it transpired that we were in a thriving networking group area, so lots of groups to possibly attend. We were also told that the job club had a membership of the local Chamber and that they had several free places at a local monthly breakfast available.

I immediately asked if I could attend as it was just down the road from home, always keeping an eye on costs as you need to. Not just when out of work, networking costs are for everyone to consider.

Another positive was that the company I had owned in the 90's had been a member of the chamber and I had also attended training courses at their facility.

> **CHAMBERS OF COMMERCE ARE A USEFUL SOURCE OF NETWORKING OPPORTUNITIES**

I was in luck as no one else felt quite ready to go out into the big imperfect world, and this became an issue that I would later raise. It seems that many of the Job Club members were given a payoff or had savings and were happy to use those to survive for a while, some even saying 6 months!

These were the people that at the meetings told the group of their inactivity since last meeting as they were still OK for money. I was not in such a position and needed to find a job quickly. After a while I stood up at the group and pointed out that this relaxed approach was of no use to them or the group, and that they were just wittering away their pension!!

A group like a job club needs to have positivity, good news and enthusiasm to build up energy that will help you push on. I soon distanced myself from these people. So, a place for me was duly booked and the event was the following Friday, so I had time to prepare myself. I had learned that the elevator pitch would not be required at the table as there would be 60+ attendees, but it could be used to start conversations, phew that was a relief on one hand and a disappointment as well.

CHAPTER THREE

THAT FIRST NETWORKING EVENT

I dusted of my suit, chose a tie from my vast collection, polished my shoes, ensured I had a pen and notebook, but at this stage no personal business cards. Having been told that exchanging of cards was an integral part of the networking scene I had asked and acquired a small number from the club on which I was able to write my details on. I entered the hotel and was directed to the room where the meeting was held. I was met by a representative of the chamber who gave me a nice plastic name badge and a list of attendees and shown where the coffee was.

I poured myself a coffee and had a glug to settle my nerves. Having never been networking before I was not sure what to do and say, so initially I found myself a quiet space and studied the guest list looking for people I might want to talk to. This is a tactic that some might find useful at events as they build their reputation.

> **STUDY THE GUEST LIST BUT DO NOT LET IT BLINKER YOU**

Nine years later and the quality of badge and guest list are still up there at the top. I have been to events where there are no guest lists, more common than you might think, and badges have varied from sticky paper label with hand written name to printed cards in holders.

I must say the chambers are the best I have come across for guests. Many member groups have magnetic ones and they are really good, I have had them for my roles at the chamber and they look good and are a fit for anyone.

> **INVEST IN A DECENT BADGE WITH YOUR NAME AND COMPANY ON**

I am still undecided on the guest list being good or bad, I suppose it is determined by how far down the journey you are. In the early days, it can be very useful to identify potential people to converse with but as I learnt it may make you dismiss some vital people because of their job titles. This is quite often the professional service people and certainly when I started they had a reputation for being dry and dusty and best avoided.

Well yes, they can be a bit staid, but others can also be a bad conversation to get involved with. What I have learnt is that you also need to see through the room. This basically means to find out who do they know, or with professional service people in particular, who are their clients? Never forget the 6 degrees of separation. This states that in 6 relationship steps you connect to almost anyone in the world!!

> ALWAYS REMEMBER TO SEE THROUGH THE ROOM

So, if you are targeted in your networking, knowing exactly who you want to meet, then these people may not be a target, but if you are clear then they may well signpost you. Many professional service people are seasoned networkers who have a good network, and this may include your target, so don't avoid them, but also do not let them take up all your time.

Also, there is likely to be some KPI's in the room!! No not key performance indicators but Key People of Influence. This is a term I came across recently in a super book by Daniel Priestley called KPI. Now I make no apologies for plugging both the book or the author, as I will be mentioning many more within these pages, because they have all helped or influenced me on my journey. Without them I basically would not be here today bashing away on a keyboard, producing what I hope is an invaluable read for many. KPI's are an invaluable group KPI's are an invaluable group and to get them into your network is a really smart move, but how are you going to do this? You first must identify them, sometimes this is easy as they are holding audience. If in doubt then ask your hosts as they will probably know, as it likely they asked them to attend in the first place.

My advice, as it is throughout this book, is that you need to be targeted and can display this in your conversation. A KPI is happy to help you if you come across well, are targeted and polite. They are more than likely to signpost you to others that may help you, they certainly will promise to do something and deliver, because that is part of how they became KPI's.

Always be targeted with your Networking

I have a reputation I am Very proud of as being someone who is giving, says they will help, then does. I also have a network of around 2000 contacts. I am no LION (LinkedIn Open Networker) and have met over 80% of my network and certainly broadcast to most regularly. So, the question is who do I, along with KPI's, know that may be able to help you? Back to that Friday morning in Slough and the next 2 hours of the event seemed to fly by, I remember a few tentative conversations, a nice cooked breakfast and a speaker presenting, but the rest is a blur of 65 suited networkers, going about their own networking activities.

What did I learn from this experience? Well despite being relieved to get home after and wind down, I realised that this was something important. Something new, and that would require effort, but I knew that I needed to sharpen up my act considerably to make it work.

Even this early I could see it may become a good place to hide and make yourself feel good. You can imagine the scenario, the one where I attended half a dozen events and spent most of the time in safe conversations. Be aware of this trap, but also don't be over hard on yourself, sometimes just being in the room is good enough. You never know who may contact you from the guest list. It is often hard to get to speak to everyone that you want to, so following up on the guest list is a clever idea. I word of caution and that is to ensure that they attended the event! The number of times I have been on a guest list but was unable to attend and then got contacted.

Usually an email would pop into my inbox and its contents would state that they were sorry we did not get a chance to talk at the event but here was a list of what they did as a service and would I be interested. Well funnily no I was not interested, as they could not even check if I attended.

I guess that they just sent everyone the same email from the guest list. Please never do this, it will not put you in a good light at all. Please do send genuinely personalised emails to non-attendees asking if they would like to meet up for a chat or to see them at the next event.

My elevator pitch back then was not doing me any favours as I had nothing to offer in the way of services or products, just a need to find work. Funnily enough including phrases like "I am out of work looking for a job" and "please can you help me?" made people rapidly move onto someone else. I am not saying that they did not want to help, but I was mostly unknown to them, so this would come across all wrong. I had not built a relationship with them, so chances of help were greatly reduced.

CHAPTER FOUR

DONE MY FIRST EVENT WHAT NOW?

With the first event done I knew I had to do more and to mix it up. So, I started up the old PC and looked on Google for other groups/events I could attend. Even though the Chamber event was free I knew that I would have to put some money aside to cover fuel and entrance costs at other events I planned to attend.

After contacting a few groups and looking on various websites it became clear that a lot of the groups allowed you to attend 2 meetings as a guest, just paying for that meeting (some were free) before they asked you to plan on joining. Joining a networking group is a major commitment in both time and money.

To extract full value for your time and money you do really need to attend as many meetings as is possible. This will give you as many opportunities as possible to make, grow and maintain those relationships, which are so crucial as well as you are getting a return on investment.

I have met a lot of people who attend a couple of events, probably network badly (through no fault of their own, my book is yet to be published!!) then claim 6 months later that it did not work for them!!

> TO NETWORK EFFECTIVELY YOU MUST PUT THE TIME AND EFFORT IN

You need to find out not only what the joining and annual fees are, but also the monthly outlay for the events. It can very easily reach a 4-figure sum, so you do need to know before you can possibly decide to commit. The thing you must consider when you have found out the annual outlay is what are you going to get in way of a return on investment. Will the room yield enough profit to cover your membership and meeting costs? Now dependent on what your offering is will determine how much businesses you need to invoice to cover theses costs.

You should know your margins before you set out, and it has been a great surprise to me how many people don't. It is a bit like in Dragons den when the people pitching at the dragons don't know their financials and the Dragons tear them to shreds. This is unforgiveable and how can you set a price for your goods or services without knowing your costs. The number of people who I have met networking who don't even pay themselves a salary is alarming. So, you need to know that if say for instance you make 25% profit on a sale, then to cover an annual outlay of £1000, you need to invoice £4000 of business to break even, where I suggest you need to double that figure to make it work.

So, the question is will the room generate this and more? If yes, go and join, if unsure then maybe not. You may have to do some more research, especially on the types of business who are members. This alone may be decisive in your decision, as if it is full of people who have limited budgets and your product or service carries a premium price, there is a miss match. Many are looking for SME and corporates who have budgets and are always looking for a good deal, so why attend a group of sole traders?

> **NETWORKING COSTS TIME AND MONEY SO YOU NEED TO BUDGET**

The next event I got myself involved in was one that is a membership group that has monthly meetings, also it had several groups across the area. If I remember rightly it was held in Beaconsfield in a big back room of a hotel. I had arrived early to meet the group leader, who in fact turned out to be the gentleman who started the networking group. He was to be a tremendous help in my early months as he took me under his wing. He let me attend meetings without paying and without a commitment to a membership fee.

He even gave me the odd lift in his trusty old Land rover. Back to Beaconsfield and my first of many of these types of meetings I attended across many different groups. The format for these breakfast events started with free networking for around 30 minutes, then sit down and an introduction from the group leader. He would start with a quick intro and then would lay out the agenda.

This was then followed by the dreaded one-minute elevator pitch. The quality of these varied from those that were timid to an extravert, who saw it as a chance to be centre stage and get a laugh, but I remember them for that not what their business did!! Also, a minute seems to range from 45 seconds to over 3 minutes!!!!

I also learnt at this early stage that a 3-minute sales pitch got what it deserved…very little. I had not changed mine at this point and I my delivery was weak and again the mentioning of looking for a job was not a great hook for those in the room. I have come to understand since, that many people do not use active listening as they are too busy rehearsing their own elevator pitch, so are only half listening, if your pitch was not an attention grabber, then it would get lost in their thoughts.

We then had a breakfast where you could continue to network with those sat near you. This part I found a lot easier to do and I am still in contact with a lady I sat next to, till this day. This was then followed by a presentation delivered by one of the group's members. This gave me time to relax but also listen to the presentation, not so much for its contents but more the delivery.

This was because I was not sure if I would have to present to a group in the future, and I wanted to be aware and learn. Finally, there was a closing speech by the group leader with updates for the members and reminders of the other groups running events locally in the upcoming weeks. This network seemed to have half a dozen groups locally and because the gentleman who set this group up was happy to "sponsor me" I attended a few more over the coming weeks.

This was no slur on this group, and I was not being disloyal, but I knew that the idea of networking was to get your message out to as many people as possible. I realised that I must attend others, and anyway, when I got into a position where I might need to network for my company, then I would have a good idea which groups were the best fit for my needs.

CHAPTER FIVE

EXECUTIVE JOB CLUB REVISITED AND NETWORK JOURNEY RAMPED UP

At the next Job Club, I told the group about my experience and whilst some were keen others seemed to be content eating into their savings. I spoke with a couple of the volunteers about the fact that doing an elevator pitch that was based around me seeking work, was not well received and I did not feel comfortable delivery it. After a brief discussion, it was agreed that I could attend representing the job club and promote them and see how it went.

This immediately felt better, and I had no issues with saying at the end of my revised elevator pitch "and I am one of those the Job club is looking to help find work". In fact, when I used it the first time I was not quite ready for the number of people who came up to me and asked questions about the club. It seems most were unaware of the job club's existence, although they had sent along people to the chamber event for a while.

This highlighted that to make networking work for you, that you had to be very clear with your elevator, you needed to follow up, basically you need to be memorable. It became easy to let people that I met know that I was one of the people the club was trying to help. It took the pressure off me and I was more confident in talking to people at events.

This got me into some good conversations, although I was grateful for the free place and the support of the job club I was mainly promoting them and not really myself. At the end of the day what I needed to do was self-promoter. I continued to attend various group meetings and started to get to know a few people. Also, I was getting to be known on the circuit, which really helped, but known for what? This was my next hurdle to overcome, I had to get people to think of me when they heard about potential openings for me.

Also, I had worked out that it was better to have a bartering tool as it was clear to me already that the more popular and what seemed more successful attendees were givers. I am a giver by nature and love to help people but what did I as an out of work manager, have to offer anyone in return for their help? Well, as I was able to attend several events a week (a benefit of being out of work!!), so I was making new relationships and building them quicker than most other networkers. This was mainly because they did not have the same amount of time as me, as they had the small matter of having to deliver work to create an income. On the other hand, my main goal at this stage was to grow a network.

I had nothing to promote or sell at this stage, but my skill in building relationships was allowing me a growing network. Whereas most networkers stayed with a particular group or in a particular area, I had no such restrictions, as long as I could afford it, I would go. Looking back on this now I see that this was a good tactic for me, but would also be for others, as it spread the size of my network geographically. This was giving me potential more opportunities for a few extra minutes' drive time.

> **DON'T STICK TO ONE GROUP OR AREA, EXPAND YOUR HORIZONS**

As I grew relationships and got to know more people I started signposting people to others. This was using my main "giving" tool to enhance my reputation. This worked well mainly because I did what I said I would do, when I said I would do it, and if I couldn't, I would let the other person know long before the deadline. I had to deliver to grow, so I saw it and still do, as the way to go about business, just in my case I was delivering Tony as a connecter.

There is a terrific book which I have, which is by Malcolm Gladwell that shows the power and influence of super connectors. In this he lays out exactly why it is so important, so again no apologies for promoting this book.

The other thing I did was to start using social media and LinkedIn. I would take peoples card offer to signpost them or at least send them a connection request. I had been shown LinkedIn by my boss back in 2007, as he was aware that I loved building relationships and in my role as a senior account director this would benefit us all. So, I had started to use it a few years earlier and had a few hundred connections.

In those days LinkedIn loved showing you the level of connection and the number of connections. So, if you had 200 people as 1st line connections who shared with their 200 connections and in turn they shared with their 200 connections, then I could theoretically be reaching 8 million people!! I will come back to LinkedIn later, but it runs hand in glove with networking, and Account management.

> SUCCESS FORMULA:- NETWORK + SOCIAL MEDIA
> AND RELATIONSHIP MANAGEMENT

CHAPTER SIX

NETWORKING GROUPS

The next break, created by my growing reputation, was that I was invited to a Business Biscotti meeting. The one thing networkers are good at is spreading the word on other events to people. If they feel that the person would benefit going but also that they would benefit the room, then they will invite them along. Now the likelihood of you having come across Business Biscotti nowadays is a lot higher than when I first discovered them.

The owners, who I got to know well, hailed from Reading and when I went to my first meeting they had around a dozen groups with attendance between 20 & 40 per meeting. This organisation sat very well with me, as they ran in a very simple format indeed. There was no official paid membership back in those days and at every venue you paid a sum for refreshments of between £2.50 and £4 dependent on venue. For someone in my position this worked well as it kept costs down and the groups were mainly local to me.

This enabled me to step up my networking and they were mainly at sociable times in good venues. I mention venues as these can be very useful to you. I started making connections with the sales and general manager of venues as I identified that they may come in useful to me going forwards. Some venues got what networking was all about and sent people along to the events. Others ignored the fact that they had a bunch of business people at their venue who they could promote the venue to, a missed opportunity or what? The one thing a lot of Micro businesses have in common is that, certainly in the early days, is that they work from home.

This means that they will use venues to meet people rather than at home. For me these venue contacts were able to help me going forwards by letting me use their facilities either for free, or at a discounted rate. In exchange, I would promote the venue to other people via Social Media or direct to my network. This enabled me to have meetings and run a few events which was a massive help.I admit I had a few favourites and built up good rapport with the staff.

There is nothing better to help your confidence in a meeting than be greeted by the staff using your name and to have the staff use it whilst you are there. I still run some events for the Chamber and I still get that good feeling of being welcomed and that they will go that extra yard for you.

> GET TO KNOW VENUE STAFF AND IN PARTICULAR THE GENERAL MANAGER

Many of you who are reading this will require to hire a room or a venue for meetings/events and having a few friendly venues will certainly help you deliver a smooth event. Believe me, having been involved in over 400 events for the chamber, a friendly and engaged staff really is a massive help. I, to this day, keep in contact with many venues as I still see that I will need them.

I am also happy to do so as I know that they will deliver for me. Another thing about building relationships with venues is that in their industry there is a constant flow of job changing, so my network of venues grows, as they move on and take me with them.

Biscotti proved to be useful on one hand and not so much on the other. I have a lot of time for Sue and Graham Reeves who are the founders and put an awful lot of time and money into this venture. I met Sue early on and immediately got on well with her. She understood my position and asked if I would help run a couple of the groups for her. I met with the lady who was the lead at both venues and instantly clicked, so I was now helping run 2 groups which had a very steady attendance figure around 35, which is a nice group size. I, personally from my experience feel that the 30-40 attendance is about right size for me. I get to complete my plan easier with this number, as I can meet new people, touch base with established connections and build on others. This allows me at the end of the event to have 2/3 business cards in my pocket, with notes on what I had promised to do for them. This then had allowed me to achieve my plan for that event.

Helping run Two groups had its advantages as I got to know the venues staff well and had a chance to meet everyone who attended. Something it is not that easy to meet all those you want to when just being an attendee. I got to meet and greet many of the attendees so that I could then target them later on at the meeting when I swopped with my hosting partner.

IF YOU HAVE THE TIME THEN OFFER TO RUN A GROUP

We ran a good event and it was soon noticed by Sue who asked me to be a roaming ambassador for her. This meant I could attend any group and not have to pay a penny, fuel costs not included, but got to know a wider spread of people and some new venue staff. I would get a message saying that a group was a lead short and go along to help.

The other benefit was going to new areas and meeting new people you also got to hear of other groups and events. I would regularly get an invite to groups that I had not been to. This again expanded my network both physically and on LinkedIn.

I also got to help launch new groups with their ambassadors. I would be involved in showing them what worked at this type of event, so it ran smoothly. Some of those I helped got it right and embraced the style of event and grew, others didn't so they never really grew their groups, which was a shame for all. Some chose venues based on the cost rather than being the right room for the group. What I had learned so far was that there are many groups across the region that have a hard core who attend regularly. Then you have the ones that come and go. I also learned that it is about building relationships and not selling. With the number of events I was able to attend and being a host at 2 highly successful groups I was able to build fast and build strong. I also topped up my contact list by adding people to my LinkedIn network, more of which later.

CHAPTER SEVEN

REINTRODUCTION TO LINKEDIN

This was all positive but was not advancing my need to get a new job. I then attended a TVCC breakfast which the speaker was going to deliver a presentation about LinkedIn. Great I thought, a chance to learn more and to apply it to help my cause. It was at this event I met the speaker Mark Pearl. He was mesmerising as he presented for 25 minutes in a manic high energy style, but the style worked for me & I could listen to him for hours.

While listening to him intently it was good to hear that I was doing some things that he spoke about, but learnt also that I needed to do a lot more. The trouble with this is that a 25-minute presentation slot is just scratching the surface, but this is often all you get to hear. I hope by the time you read this book to be delivering 1-2-1 and small group training which is tailored to people's needs. I took the chance after the event to catch him after he had been besieged by the audience. I explained my situation to him and he understood the situation I was in and what I was trying to achieve. He gave me some more tips there and then, and told me to link in with him and he would appraise my profile. I left feeling that this may be a break through moment.

When I got back to my home office I immediately sent Mark a personalised connection request. I say home office, as I was treating finding a job as a full-time role and would dress appropriately and follow a plan and a budget. My wife knew that if I was at that desk then I was working. I would strongly suggest that if you use a home office that you take a similar stance as you must be disciplined and professional as it is too easy to be distracted.

Mark soon after accepted my request and a few days later he sent me a critique. I read it thoroughly and was pleased to see that I was doing some things right already, in fact it was not too shabby. There were things I could be doing to improve my profile, things that will pull people towards me. Also, he showed me how to use certain parts of the platform to search for people and companies and how to make a connection request far more likely to be accepted.

He said that he was happy to help me as he knew I would spread the word and he mainly dealt with high end companies in UK and across Europe, so was unlikely to run into each other in the market. Eight years later I can confirm he was correct and that not that many people had heard of him when I mentioned him, because of the circles he operated in. Those that did know him would only sing his praises. This relationship and help was a nice advantage for me and he continues to help me to this day, in fact I will be having lunch with him to discuss the book, so some last- minute tweaks may be on the cards.

USE LINKEDIN TO NETWORK ONLINE

I applied his teachings and got my profile to be "All Star" rated so I knew if people found me in a search then It would reflect me and look professional. It also had made me more likely to come up in searches. For example, as I write this if you search for "networking", I am 21st out of 10.9 million!! Also, I know how to move that figure into the top 10.

How useful is that if you are trying to attract people to your profile? It is like most things we search for on Google, we never usually look beyond the first page. So, with 25million users in the UK LinkedIn is the main B2B professional network and a terrific way of keeping on top of relationships and being found by potential clients.

The time and effort I took to work on my profile and refine it has repaid itself time and time again. This along with my growing networking reputation, made me a well-known person on the circuit. Along with my disposition to help people, this got me a reputation as one of the most connected people in the area! I don't believe that to be true, but people were saying it on a regular basis.

My network would introduce me like this, "have you met Tony yet, he knows everyone?" Also, on more than one occasion I had people come up to me and tell me that they knew about me and had heard my name mentioned many times on the circuit.

> **SPEND TIME GETTING YOUR LINKEDIN PROFILE AS GOOD AS YOU CAN**

Now all this is great, and I am told that many people would love to have my network, which is useful but, was it working for me.......in a word NO!! The reason it was not working correctly for me was clearly someone's fault, and that someone is me.

I have always accepted responsibility as I believe that in most situations you have control of the way you react. It is true that I had a nice size network and a good reputation, but ultimately, why was I networking?

Well I knew it was to find a job or an opportunity, but I was not telling people this on a regular basis!! Why was this? Well basically the next part of this book will answer this and explain how I made some big mistakes over the first six months.

The question "why?" is a very powerful one and Simon Sinek explains its importance with his bestselling "Start with Why. I so believe that the contents of Simon's book are so powerful that I lent it to my CEO to read, as I was not clear on the companies' real "Why".

> **KNOW YOUR WHY?**

CHAPTER EIGHT

NETWORKING IS GOOD BUT

So, I had settled into the networking world and was slowly growing my network, but no as yet no sniff of a job. I thought I was doing well but the friendliness and routine of the networking had lulled me into a false state of mind. Networking when you are on your own, employed or not, is a wonderful way of staying sane. The regular contact with business people the friendly smiling faces, the buzz, all made it a good place to be.

I cannot imagine running a small business without this support network, they became a replacement for work colleagues. I know some people will scoff at this but being a very sociable person, this really helped me, and I know talking to others that it has helped them to. Yes, ultimately, we all needed to sell something, for me it was myself for employment.

The thing is that just being around others was both comforting and inspiring. There is a big culture of help, and there was great advice and support offered within the networking ranks. I had become detached from my main goal and a little bit comfortable, which was dangerous. After a while of being part of the networking scene, things did change and people I had known for a while tried to help me. They could see that I was always prepared to give so some started offering me commission for selling their products and services.

Also, some associate roles opened up for me, and again this was down to the effort I had put in. People were now happy to take a chance on me, and often the reason was the network I had built and the reputation I had for delivering. I believe also that they wanted to help me, but as I was not sending our clear messages on what help I needed, they decided that what they offered would help me.

This looking back was very kind of them, but on the flip side I am also sure that some just used me as a free salesperson/advocate. Trouble is, when you are down on your luck, any act of perceived kindness was taken as real.

This also gave me a feeling of belonging, which when you are 6 months into redundancy with no savings and the mortgage insurance just about to run out, is a good feeling. Trouble was is that it also started making me desperate, enough to look at anything put in front of me.

So, I duly spent 3 months trying to get people interested in other people's products. Looking back this was a massive mistake and waste of time. I had gone from this nice chap with the great network looking for an employment opportunity, to a...... well even now I am not sure what!! What I am now sure of is that my network was clueless how to help me.

My network wanted to be supportive but were now even more confused about me and exactly what I wanted from them in the way of help and support. This was a disaster, I had got to the point that my network now included a lot of people happy to be my unpaid salesforce (people who are very happy to promote you to others with no expectations in return).

Trouble was they had no idea what I was going to walk into the room with at the next event and how they could help me with this. Looking back at that period and the things I got myself involved in, most things where to niche for my network.

They were not really the target audience and the only thing that I thought really worked, people did not get!! This was QR codes, and these could be used by a lot of people I networked with, and were not expensive. Ironically, they are used a lot more these days and if they had adopted them they would have put us both ahead of the curve. I even had a product that, once scanned would point the user to a website that contained a short promotional video, which would now be cool.

Along with this as a promotional aid for me I had a business card made up. This card had my name on one side and on the other a QR code which linked through to my LinkedIn profile. This enabled people to find out a lot more about me than I could ever get on a business card.

I had software to create the codes and personalise them, but people just did not get it and thought it was a passing technology. I will have a QR codes within the covers of this book which will lead to various bonus material and information. I still think there is a place for them in my life.

SPEND TIME GETTING YOUR LINKEDIN PROFILE AS GOOD AS YOU CAN

I had software to create the codes and personalise them, but people just did not get it and thought it was a passing technology. I will have a QR codes within the covers of this book which will lead to various bonus material and information. I still think there is a place for them in my life.

Well as I stated above the QR idea did not resonate along with the other things I was promoting which was a big cause of concern for me at the time. Luckily a friend within my network sat me down and pointed out the problem in very simple terms.

Most people in the networking world that had met me thought I was a great guy and one they would happily help, but most had no idea how they could help. I was slightly taken back by this comment, but they followed it up by saying that I was across so inconsistent.

I would almost have a new product or service to talk about each time they met me. I was confusing them so much that they had no idea how to help me. I was not being targeted with my networking and actually I was virtually wasting my time and effort with these new ideas.

BE TARGETED WITH YOUR NETWORKING

Now this big mistake has become one of things I make clear to avoid to others. When I meet a new person out networking, and they are not all newbies, I tell them that they really need to be targeted when they go networking. Even to the point that you know your target down to the person you want to get connected to.

Networkers generally enjoy helping others, but if you don't tell them what you want how can they help you? For example, If someone comes up to me networking and tells me they want to meet a partner in a professional service company based in Reading, then I can help.

I will do this by signposting them to 2 or 3 people within my network. Whereas, which is much more common, they will say they want to meet someone or anyone that.... I immediately cannot help them and stop them there and then. I explain that I don't have the time to try and get more details from them or second guess their actual needs. This seems really harsh, but I immediately tell them why they need to be targeted, some get it some don't. I am not the only one with this dilemma, most regulars, and especially KPI's have the same issue, they would love to help but they need more to go on.

This of course was exactly what I was doing for so long, and I now clearly understand my networks frustration at the lack of targeting that I went networking with. Being everything to everyone does not work, especially at the Micro business end, you need to find a niche and own it.

FIND YOUR NICHE AND OWN IT

This made me sit down and reassess my plans, and whilst I was doing this I realised my second big mistake. I was not networking in the right space!! I knew that I had to get the security of an employed job and the regular salary that it brings. I could not do a commission only job, nor did I have enough money to have a go setting up on my own.

This is when I sat and looked at the groups I attended and realised a lot of them were just not right. That was because they were mainly consistent of micro businesses, which while very supportive of me and willing to help, were never really in a position to employ me on a full-time salary. I will again point out that you need to "see through the room" and look at their networks, were they consisting of any companies big enough to take on a full-time salary? I am sure that there was some, but I never unearthed any. Therefore, this did greatly reduce the effectiveness of networking at a lot of the groups that I attended. They were just very unlikely to be able to help me in my main aim of finding full time employment.

> **MAKE SURE YOU ARE IN THE RIGHT ROOM**

The trouble is that they are all looking to get work from bigger companies, so you are unlikely to be top of their priority list. Understandable, but not that much use to you. There is always an upside to everything and that is if you have been very targeted, then the chances of your name coming into conversation is greatly improved.

This will only happen when they trust you, which takes time and good relationship building skills. I certainly do know that seeing through the room works, and I have seen and heard of some very good outcomes from referrals/signposting. Trouble was none were for employment, they were winning work from the larger company they had been referred to. It was now very apparent that with these two big mistakes that I needed a new plan and fast.

> **REGULARLY REVIEW YOUR PLANS,
> ARE YOU ON TRACK?**

CHAPTER NINE

REVIEW AND MOVE FORWARDS

I decided to analyse all the regular groups I attended to see what the plus and minus points were against my target of a salaried position. I was very honest in my appraisal of what opportunities for full time work they could bring. This mainly boiled down to the people in the room, hence the "All about the room book title". I found myself in the situation I mentioned earlier in the book. I was weighing up whether to continue going to a group based on the end result I sought. I then judged which rooms I needed to be in and how often. I needed to be in the right room, meeting the right people so some groups were just not viable anymore. I was time rich but alas funds poor, which also helped to concentrate the mind.

So, some groups had to be dropped, after all I had dwindling reserves of money, so needed to make the best use of it. t was a hard decision to stop going to some groups where I had built up good friendship, but I had realised that friendship would not pay the bills. Other groups I had to cut back on and, I needed to discover some new groups that were more likely to have more of the right people in the room. So, to analyse the previous months networking activities, I had been in the wrong rooms talking to the wrong people.

Also, I had been confusing them as well, so they could not help me even if they wanted to. Looking back, I understand how easy it was for this to happen and I am sure it would be the same for many others. This is one of the driving reasons for me starting to write this book.

The brutal truth was that a large part of those previous months had been wasted in regard to my main target of finding myself a job. This time had been very useful in other ways which have helped me a lot since. So not a total waste, but it was not helping me achieve my target at the time, namely that full time role.

> BE HONEST WITH YOURSELF

I had been naïve and thought because I found that I could build relationships quickly and people warmed to me, that I was being successful. This will not be the case for everyone, and I had a good grounding from my account directorship days that not everyone will have. The support that you get from networking is not just in the advice and signposting. It goes deeper than that in that it is actually feeling that you belong to something.

Now I know some people are happy with their own company and though I was comfortable with my own company, we are social animals. So please don't discount the companionship that networking brings, it can be the difference between feeling alone and helpless to feeling part of something. The benefit of the association is having the extra confidence that belonging inspires in you.

There must be a balance, and I liken myself to someone who is a sole trader. It can get lonely, so networking provides some social interaction laced with opportunities to start, maintain and build those relationships. I know that I will bang the LinkedIn drum throughout this book, but it really is such a great tool to maintain these relationships.

People still buy from people, even if it is only you that you are selling. You need to be alert as you will find yourself in such a position at any time. You don't have to be at an organised event to find yourself networking with people and they don't have to be dressed in business attire.

So, I needed to look at my activities and my plans in detail. What groups were working for me, which was not so easy as I did not really have any Metrix in place. I suggest that Metrix are not easy to implement but if you can, then do it as it makes things easier to monitor.

The Metrix can take the shape of a sales pipeline/funnel, seeing where you are with the people you meet, so you know how to interact with them. In fact, a basic CRM, commonly known as a spreadsheet would work well. You could see where you are in the relationship and if it would be worth continuing to the next level.

If I had done this a lot of people would be in the category of keeping in touch on LinkedIn with the occasional event meeting. Some would have had a NFA against them, others would be highlighted so that I could see those I needed to get in touch with. This then could be put into your event attendance strategy along with other factors. I have included a link to download the spreadsheet at the end of the book.

> **APPLY METRICS TO YOUR ACTIVITIES AND STUDY THE RESULTS**

You will find that there are a few groups where regular attendance will be essential, whereas others you will find that every quarter may suffice to keep your name in their consciousness. To show an example of this, I was pleasantly surprised in early 2017.

After not really networking for about a year outside the chamber events that I ran that I was still remembered. I attended an event in Ascot that people who I had not physically met for 2/3 years came up to me and said hello.

Even though that had not met me in years they immediately recognised me, and many told me they were following me on Social Media. So, if you connect correctly and make the right impression, then you can live in the memory for quite a while. It also helps if you are constantly reaching out on SM.

CHAPTER TEN

ACRONYMS AND CLICHES AND FURTHER PLANNING

I have deliberately used acronyms in that last sentence of the previous chapter to make a point, and that is DON'T use them. You are assuming the other person/s knows what you are on about. All well and good if they do, but what about those who don't? they may lose the thread of what you are saying, lose interest, feel embarrassed that they don't know, or just think you are showing off.

So, to correct my mistake CRM, is a customer relationship management tool, NFA is, no further action and SM is social media. Never assume that the person knows what they mean otherwise you will find yourself fulfilling the old Benny Hill sketch, in that to assume you make an ASS of U and ME.

> AVOID USING ACRONYMS, IT IS NOT BIG OR CLEVER

Back to the plan, which I believe would really mirror how you would market your business (it as I have said before that for some readers, your business is looking for opportunities). A friend and sometime TV star Richard Woods runs a very good marketing agency and has written a terrific book called the Digital Trailblazer.

He also runs some great seminars where he demonstrates how his company market in diverse ways and take Metrix. This means they record data over a set period then chose the ones that work and drop those that don't.

He points out in his book it will not be the same for all people/businesses, but why keep doing things that don't work and cost you money? I love the old saying "If you always do what you always did you will always get what you always got" so if that is a poor result then stop doing it. Stop lying to yourself that one day it will come good, because for the majority of cases, it won't.

> **IF IT IS NOT WORKING THEN STOP DOING IT**

So, whilst I recall some good old clichés I might as well use a couple more of my favourites, as they are relevant to business. One is the 5 "P's", Prior Planning Prevents Poor Performance (there is a 6 "P" version but let's keep it clean). The other is "fail to plan, plan to fail". I won't apologise that they have been around a long time but the truth is they don't date and are both well worth remembering.

So now that you have stepped back and planned your next few weeks/months strategy you need to take action. Planning and not taking action is a disaster, so action you must take. A good plan for a networking event would be to start new conversations, top up others and confirm some as well. Over a 2-hour event with networking,

I would try and have 5 or 6 new conversations with the target of leaving with 3 Business cards and 3 promises from me to take action. That is the most important goal, but you should also try to speak to 3 or 4 people that you have started a relationship with and that you want to build.

Finally, the easy one and that is touching base with the confirmed connections say 2 or 3. That is quite a tall order to do in 2 hours as some will be lost to speakers etc so you may have 90 minutes to do (max on the plan) 13 conversations. That is barely 7 minutes each, so you definitely do not want to be in with a time bandit for long. At the minimum, I would like 3 new conversations, 3 top ups and 3 confirmed ones.

> **YOU NEED A PLAN AND YOU NEED TO STUDY THE RESULTS AGAINST IT**

I used to carry a notebook and pen as well as a modest supply of business cards, and would make notes prior to the event. Then when there I would add to them within the first 10 minutes of arriving when I have scoped the room. As I then began networking I would continue to make notes as conversations finished, either on the business card you have asked for or in my book.

I find this plan works for me. If I ask a person for their card I will also ask if it is OK to make notes on their card. If not, then in your notebook if the card has nowhere to make notes. The writing of the note in front of them is strong, as it confirms in their mind that you will do as you have promised.

Also, if you know me or I have told you, that where I put the card in my jacket determines what I do with it. Most cards that I ask for will go in my right-side jacket pocket. But, if it is urgent, it will go in my breast pocket, but if it goes in my left pocket that is bad. Because it will end up in file 13, AKA the bin. Now this is my own doing and helps remind me what I need to do.

Some people will say that they keep all cards, which is fine, but I do wonder if they ever follow up all the cards, my guess is not. If I ask for a card it is because I have promised to do something for you, or we have an instant symmetry. If I am given a card without asking I will accept, as I don't want to appear to be rude, but the likelihood is I may not be in contact. This is what I do, but I suggest you do what is comfortable for you.

> **MAKE SURE YOU ALWAYS CARRY SUPPLIES OF YOUR BUSINESS CARD**

Also, if I get asked for my card (but again it is my way) I won't always oblige. Because of this I do not give out many cards at events.

The reason is that if I saw this relationship moving forward I would normally ask for their card. Therefore, there is no need for them to have my card, as I will be taking action and contacting them very soon. This way they will get my details from the email I send to them.

What I don't want is people adding me to a mailing list because they have my card then spamming me. This sounds bad but believe me people will, it is their idea of marketing!!. It may seem arrogant, but these cards cost me money as does the time I have spent at an event, so if I don't see a need then I won't hand them out.

This way I may miss out on some people signposting people towards me, but I have a 2000 strong network that I interact with which I feel is the right number for my circumstances.

This figure was not preconceived but a figure I just came to naturally. I still add people, but I also audit my connections from time to time and do delete some. This may be because they have left the area, changed jobs, or just have not interacted since connecting. Again, this is what suits me, but could well be different for you, I just think it is something to be considered. I think in the early days it is a good idea to take everyone's card who offers it to you, until you have built a decent size network. I will now often take a card from someone just because they have a niche that my network does not cover sufficiently or that I know will be useful to my network. Bottom line is that I see networking at events something I need to do to help with my marketing plan, so I have costed it into my budget.

BUDGET FOR YOUR NETWORKING ACTIVITIES

I often challenge people at event with a few questions that are meant to make them think. I am trying to help them by reminding them why they are there, and this is after I have extracted the reason for their presence. Mostly this revolves around promoting their business or if they don't get how to network, trying to sell. So, I think these are both business activities, so should be costed. I will ask that what they want to get out of the event then point out that they should be allowing £100/hour for their time.

That is not their hourly rate but the value they should put on themselves and their business. This often makes them take a step back and think, and often they will get a bit more serious as they had not considered this.

There are obvious exceptions to this and that is fine, I have often gone to an event just to be sociable or support a connection. Also, if it is outside normal working hours then again you can take a more relaxed approach if you want.

I often find that I just naturally network, my instincts kick in and I see an opportunity to help or add to my network and I just go into the mode. You may also find that because the pressure is off you that opportunities appear without trying.

I have found that the more informal an event amongst business people the better the flow of conversation and information. Meet these people in a structured networking business event and they are in that mode, or should be, so things are not so laid back and they are more serious.

It is almost as if people's guards are down at social events, they are not there on business (yes, I know you are always representing your business). Even at social events one likely question you will get asked is "what do you do for a living?"

These social events are also a terrific way to build relationships by finding out other things about your connections. They will often talk about more personal or family matters and you can then refer to this at an appropriate later date to further cement the relationship.

SOCIAL EVENTS ARE ALSO NETWORKING OPPORTUNITIES

A seasoned networker/relationship builder can often get the personal, family information at any event, but beware do not think you can in the early days. I pride myself at how quick I can get a relationship established, and my ability to extract those little gems of personal or family information. I can then use this information to cement the relationship to both of ours benefit.

I must warn you that this takes time and lots of practice, because like most things that people make look easy, there are hundreds of hours of practice behind it. I am a completely different person now to the one I was back when I was working 10 years ago. I was fairly shy and conservative, but soon learned that this would not get me anywhere in networking.

So, I invested time and a small amount of money in acquiring the skills I needed, but it is practice in the real-world situation that hones the skill. If you see seasoned networkers at an event then try and get to talk to them, the majority and more than happy to help you as it is in their nature.

Adding them as a new person to your network will enhance it, and for them connecting a person who is new to the networking world can only be a good thing. They are of course looking to help but also to see who you know, they will be looking through the room.

The true networking experts will happily give without wishing to receive, but there is a small percentage who are only worried about what is in it for them and play the short game, not the long one. That is fine, it takes all sorts, but you can often gauge people from the first interaction. If not sure then ask someone about them, we all have networking reputations.

> **DON'T BE SCARED TO ASK YOUR NETWORK QUESTIONS**

CHAPTER ELEVEN

DO YOUR MARKET RESEARCH

The next stage for your networking plan is to try all the groups and as I have said earlier you will find that many just don't work for you. Give them all a chance, but if the room just does not seem right for you then please move on. There are lots of different organisations who have networking groups countrywide whereas some are regional. Even groups from the same organisation can vary widely, it is all back to that saying, "it's the room that counts".

Increasingly there are companies and some venues that run their own events on a regular basis. These are often professional service companies and they lay on a good spread and have a satisfactory level of attendance in both numbers and the position of many of the attendees. More often than not they are at their premises and often they will be closer to working hours or even during the working day. They rarely charge so are a useful source of new connections without too much layout.

> **NETWORK AT COMPANIES OFFICES ARE WELL WORTH ATTENDING**

As I say some venues cotton on to the exposure they get from hosting a networking group so will often decide to host their own. The one I have attended recently was at Ascot racecourse and it has attendances in 3 figures, with lots of their staff mingling with the attendees promoting the venue and its services. No one minds as the feast and drinks they lay on is exceptional.

The impression they make works as I was happy to signpost Richard Woods to the venue as he had told me that he was looking for a potential change of venue, as his seminar was growing in size. This time it came to nothing but certainly raised my profile with the venue and fulfilled what Richard wanted from me as he knew that in the region I had a very powerful black book of venue contacts.

Venue's sales and general managers are good connections to have for most if not particularly for the jobhunters. If your business ever needs a venue for any event or meeting, it is far easier if you have a contact or that you can name drop. Also, due to the hospitality industries trend of moving every 2/3 years (seen as not being ambitious enough if they stay longer), whether within the company's venues or to the opposition, gives you more opportunities.

This is because if you have built a good connection with them, then they will take you with them, and will be keen to offer the new venues facilities to you. The replacements are also a good people to get connected to as they will often want to continue, if not better the venue offering to you. There are always the ones that don't get Networking and the relationship therefore is not as good as before. An example of this is that I had a really good relationship with a local racecourse.

So, when I decided to run a full day's seminar locally, they were my first choice. Unfortunately, when I reached the point of looking to reserve a date my 2 connections had moved on. I did ask for an introduction to the new contact, but they did not have that relationship with me, so the venue was no longer top of my list. One of my contacts had gone to a rival racecourse but this was 35 miles away and not ideal location wise. I am still considering them as my contact is bending over backwards to accommodate my needs.

Also, the staff that look after you on the night, while not likely to be networking connections, can be invaluable if you treat them correctly. They will look after you, and will therefore of course let any new Manager know what a good person you are and that doing business with you is worthwhile. I am a firm believer that if you treat all people you meet as equals and be polite, it can only work in your favour. This can be useful when you need to meet up with a potential client or hold an important meeting. Firstly, the availability of a room or quiet space is easier found and the service you and your guests receive will be elevated.

In fact, I often get asked to pop in when in the area, and when I don't I get an email or call asking why I have not been in to see them (good account management from them). That is because they genuinely like you and want to maintain the relationship. Also, there will be times when you need a space to work yourself and going to a friendly venue with a warm welcome really does benefit you. I have some venues that will give me free rooms, free coffee or offer discounts on larger ticket items not usually offered to the public. One of the main reasons that I get this treatment is that I freely promote the venue at the events and particularly on social media. So, embrace the different networking that can be had, plan ahead but be flexible as you do not know where a conversation may take you.

As you get established in the networking family you will get to hear about new events that are spread by word of mouth and that you need an introduction to get in. Again, I say go and suss out the room and its potential, and if it looks promising try to get to ingratiate yourself with the organisers so that you are welcomed back. Some events you get a negative feel for and you want to get out as soon as possible.

There are always ways to leave an event but do be polite. I have left a few events when it was obvious that it was not a fit with my targets. Why waste time when you don't have to, just learn the lesson and move on. It is all about fit and one popular style of event that just does not fit with me is speed networking. Lots of people like it and you must try it if offered but I like to build relationships and this forced method is just not for me. I need more than the few minutes to interact with someone for either of us to get anything out of it. This next section is taken from a series of blogs I did recently and is aimed at giving hints and tips on various aspects of networking.

> READ THE NEXT SECTION THEN COME BACK TO IT AS A REFERENCE GUIDE

CHAPTER TWELVE

NETWORKING BLOGS

Why Network these days?

I started Networking 10 years ago and I have seen many changes to the local scene. Lots of new groups popped up and in time a lot disappeared. You could almost network continually all day so many were there. I had my reasons as to why I got involved and there is a story there I will tell in time. What I found was a lot of people very keen to tell you about their business, and not overly keen on listening to what you did.

The groups ranged in size from 12-100 and their frequency varied as well. It felt like a fantastic way to meet new people, but I did learn that to build a proper network was to have a plan for before, during and after any event, and NO, collecting a handful of business cards was not a successful outcome at all.

I intend to write a series of blogs on how I discovered the right way to do things and by passing on my experience, hope to stop people making mistakes that I did. Yes, I did make mistakes because when I Started there was no real training involved, which is another thing I aim to change by running a series of workshops. These workshops will not be me just telling, the only way to truly learn I believe is by being involved.

So back to my question of "why network" and the answer will vary dependant on who it is, but I believe everyone should network, but it must be planned and allowed for in any marketing budget you have.

The one main reason is to build trusted relationships.... yes, trusted relationships, not to sell, this will come about naturally when you have been networking properly for a while. I have a network across my area who freely refer me and even after years of no physical contact treat me like an old friend. Want to know how? well, that I will reveal in a series of 12 Blogs

Been advised to network what shall I do? There comes a time in most business people's careers when networking is on the to do list, be it for yourself or you have been asked to by your current employer, and you just do not know what to do. This happened to me back in 2008 when at the age of 48 I became out of work. It had been years since I had to look for a job from the position of being "on the dole"!

Talk about being out of touch, I was out of my depth. Luckily, I found an executive job club who advised me that one thing I would have to do was network. So, that is what I did, I scoured the internet to find events and then spent 6 months basically networking badly!! The reason was that I did not really know why I was there and what to do, I had no plan.

Yes, networking is working and therefore there is a cost involved in both time and money. My first event was with a group locally that had 70 business people attending. I had all the feelings everyone else has, nerves, fear etc. but I lasted the 2 hours. This was the start of my networking career and although scary I knew it was essential.

Looking back now at those nervous beginnings it brings a smile to my face, as I have learnt so much and built such a useful network, that those first 6 months of bungling along now seem funny. There was little network training being offered, and that is largely still true, so I do feel sorry for people setting out on their networking career.

Top tip, know why you are there

The first tip and probably the best one is to be totally sure of why you are going, what your target markets are how many good conversations you are going to have. Networking is not a game of who can collect the most cards, if you think it is, then I am sorry you will never be really successful. Successful networkers go to an event to see who they can help, what relationships they can move forward, and who is new on the block.

So, to help those nerves and to get some results go with a plan, and make it measurable, which normally means what follow ups can you arrange. You then go with a purpose and are accountable to yourself to get the desired outputs.

Networking for the first time

This is the big one, well it was for me, as even if you have This is the big one, well it was for me, as even if you have planned as in my last blog, you will still be confronted by complete strangers, and not be sure what to do.

Types of events available to you

Some groups will issue guest lists in advance, but this is rare and unlikely, more likely is that you will be given a badge and a guest list on arrival. This is normally the first pleasant surprise as I have been to very few events where I have not found the person on the desk to have been really friendly.

A tip here is to always wear your badge on your right lapel/side! Also, if you get a guest list then scan it and mark off a few targets (because you have planned, ahead haven't you?). Why right side for badge you may enquire, well when you go to shake hands (right hand) you pivot towards the person and the badge comes into their line of sight where on the left (easier as suits have a breast pocket) will take your badge away (not very memorable and in some cultures rude).

Deep breath and remember the plan

So now enter the room with you badge proudly displayed and a plan in your head. Often drinks are part of the initial reception/networking and people naturally gravitate towards them. Now this is when the magic happens more often than not, and a person next to you in the queue or after you have got your drink will approach you and ask you a question.

Yes, there is no need to stand alone looking sheepishly at other groups in full flow, there is very likely to be some top-level networkers there who will take it as part of their role to get you involved. If this does not happen after a short while, then you do need to make a move. Go for a group of 3 or more who have open stances allowing easy access for others to join.

Never try and join a couple who are standing squarely opposite each other. Networking etiquette is a whole blog on its own, so look out for it in my series.

Your first group interaction

Once joined a group you will get asked who you are, what you do etc. so be prepared for this, but do not deliver an elevator pitch, it will be spotted. In fact, I found the best thing was to turn it back on them asking them who and what. They will be more than happy to tell you and listen to what they say, not what you want to say.

To truly listen and to show that you understand, will elevate your status. Also by finding out what they do you can gauge how much you need to engage with them. Are they the type of person you had planned to speak to?

In Summary:

So, like most things, it gets better with practice, but if you go with a plan and a clear idea of you target market you are already ahead of 75% of the room, so there is no need to fear networking first time, just do it, but do it with a plan and realistic expectations.

2 tried and tested ways to ensure you don't waste your time networking

Your time is precious. You know this. I know this. Particularly when you are new to networking, it can feel good to be out there doing stuff. However, networking is often an illusion. It can suck away all your precious time, with often very little return. This article looks at how to make sure that when you are networking, particularly working the room, you do so in a way to make the best use of your time.

Look at the schedule and plan

Most events with networking have a schedule so you can see how much time there is for networking. Knowing this you must use this time effectively and not have it wasted. There are many types of events that you can attend and almost all of them have an element of free networking. I say free because you can circulate freely, as opposed to where you are sat on a table only able to speak easily to the people on either side of you.

So, find out what type of event it is and how much time you have for free networking and then plan the minimum number of effective conversations to call the event a success.

Remove yourself politely from the hard sell folk

So, you have a plan and go with best intentions, but not everyone has the same outlook. There is almost always at least one person who is there to hard sell. You will get to know the type and even their names after a while. However, until you know to avoid these people, you will get caught in that conversation that you don't want to be in. This conversation will be painful and also a waste your precious networking time.

Time to get out of it!

The best way to exit this is to listen for a while and then ask a question that is a pattern interrupt. This means it is not expected but is relevant. It will throw them off guard and allow you to exit the situation. Easiest one is to ask them is have they been before? Is it a good group?

Do they like the venue etc. They are likely to say something positive which you latch onto, such as they say the coffee is good, so you then have your out, "I had better go and have one, thanks for the tip".

Sometimes there is no hook so the one's I used were "Had we better not move on, so we get a chance to talk to more people?" or "I have just spotted someone I need to speak to, thanks for the info". Both are non-offensive and give you that out.

If you are lucky and further into your networking journey, a seasoned networker will bail you out, because they know the person you are talking to is a time bandit, and they want you to get the best experience.

In summary

So, remember time is money and try to get out of the "wrong" conversation and hit your pre-event goals.

What to take

Taking the correct items with you really depends on the type of event so if not sure ask the organisers what is allowed at the event as it can vary dependant on the host.

The essentials

The golden rule of Networking is to ensure you have enough Business cards with you. You need enough to hand out but please do not hand them out like confetti. I have seen some appalling bad etiquette over the years, with one that sticks in the mind that happened at a Morning event in Wokingham.

There was a group of us talking in a closed circle (more about types of groups in a later blog), and two people we had never seen before literally pushed into the circle, interrupted the person speaking and handed out a card and a A5 leaflet, then without an apology walked off to harass another group. What do you think happened to the card and leaflet?...........they were all cast into a bin because of the way they were handed out.

It is OK to take some literature, and some events will even have a table to display them, but in all honestly there is little point in the early days of networking, displaying them on a table, as you don't want to have to man the table.

Clothing etiquette

Another aspect is what to wear to the event, but be aware you are promoting you the brand, so what image do you want to portray? Even at the casual end dress as the brand ambassador for you. Some people I have met over the years have a very strong Brand identity and will wear colours that reflect this. For a gentleman that is often the Tie, for ladies the dress Certainly, at more formal events full business attire is required, and I always had cufflinks and a tie pin to look as smart as I could.

In summary:

So, remember you are representing yourself or your company and first impressions do count so make the effort to be remembered for the right reasons as networking is a long-term marketing plan so ensure the impression you leave is positive

Business Card

I have in a previous blog, told you that a good supply of cards at an event is essential, but what type of card and what should it contain and how should it be presented are also quite important.

You don't get a second chance to make a first impression Again, if you are in control of getting your cards made then remember it is part of your branding. The point of giving someone your card is that you are passing them information so that they can remember you, so you should ensure that as well as you and your companies name, you have your contact details such as email address, office and mobile number.

Dependent on space you can also add your twitter handle and LinkedIn profile details, but make it too busy. In this day and digital age, there is no need to put an address, but if you work in a geographically defined area then you could add that, I used to have Thames Valley on mine for instance.

The back of the card is an area when there are a few trains of thought, but the one I think is most useful is to either leave blank or add areas for the recipient to write, so things such as Date, venue, note are good prompts. The card itself will be added to a collection by the person who you give it to, so you need to ensure it is decent quality.

I have been given cards that look like the person printed them at home to ones that linger in my mind years after receiving them. Your card is part of your brand so even when setting out it needs to be excellent quality, so invest in decent quality and remember that if you intend the back to be written on, ensure that it can be and is not gloss!!

Card Etiquette

I would always ask the person who gave me their card permission to write on the back, as it shows respect and if I have taken their card it is because I have promised to do something for them. If you take up this idea then you must absolutely carry through your promise as this is all about reputation building, and I have acquired the desired reputation of someone who is a person of their word. This is very powerful, because the likely hood of you being referred is a lot higher. I have been networking for 10 years and I have got to a point that when I attend networking events, my unpaid salesforce and reputation allow me the luxury of people coming up to me rather than me going to start conversations.

In Summary:

So, for those starting out your business card is vital, because that is the thing people take away from the event and it is that which reminds people about you. So, invest a little money and give the right impression from the start.

The novice networker's guide to starting a conversation

So, you have arrived at the event, with your plan and your business cards, but what do you say? How do you start a conversation?

Getting the formalities out of the way

There will be more than likely a reception desk where there your hosts will greet you and hand out some event related items. These could be Badges, Guest List or vouchers for refreshment

Use your first question to test the water

I found out that the best way for me, once the formalities were out of the way, I would ask the first question. I did this, so I could determine how long I should be in this conversation. In the early days initially just talking to someone was a relief. However, as I got more experiencedI would use the first question technique. This is where you ask the first question, which is typically a safe and simple question. Think of it was the networkers equivalent of small talk. Say something like, have you been to this group before? What brings you here? or the obvious, what do you do for a living?

People love talking about themselves and their business

Almost all peoples' favourite subject and the one they feel most at home talking about is themselves and what they do. Listen to what they say, rather than think about what you want to say. Does what they do sound something that could be of interest to you, are they a potential client for you?

This is highly unlikely on first meeting. So, a more realistic objective for the conversation is to find out whether they could be a referrer for you, or know someone who could be a target for you.

It's all about who they know

One lesson I learnt was that it is not always the person in front of you that is important, it is who they know. For me professional service people had a reputation for being dull and of little use. But their client base, that is another story! Just think who the accountants, lawyers and financial advisors have in their client base.

I'm sure at least one of their clients would be advantageous for you to meet. Think about how you can uncover a little more about their client base. E.g. "Who is an ideal client for you?", "What's on your desk right now?", "What parts of your client base are you seeing the most growth in right now?'

In summary:

So, ask that first question and try to follow your plan. I would say a 2-hour event that yields 3 or 4 promised follow ups is a success, but in the beginning just a single promise to meet up for coffee is a great start.

Setting expectations

You are concerned that you do not get instant returns on the time and money you have invested. I want to be very honest with you and say that to network effectively on a regular basis is going to take around 6 months, so you need to put the effort in to build those relationships. I have seen people meet for the first time and business has resulted from this, I am also proud to say that as sign poster I have put people together that has resulted in business.

This second scenario is way more likely as in a way I have done the initial hard work for you. Going with an open mind, an open ear and realistic expectations will enable you to leave the event having thought it has been a success. Going with the aim to sell, will mainly lead to disappointment.

The whole point of networking is to build up relationships with lots of people to the point where trust becomes part of the relationship, because without trust, the relationship is going nowhere.

Helping others should be a primary plan

I mainly signpost people to people who I think it is worth their time talking to, I do not refer as I strongly believe that to refer then the person needs to have done paid work for me that I was happy with. For me this is only a handful of people, but signposting wise I have many in all different fields that I am happy for people to contact and use my name.

Reputation is everything and anyone who refers someone else is putting that reputation on the line. If the person does not deliver, then you lose part of that hard thought for reputation.

In Summary:

The bottom line is about building a reputation amongst the networking community, delivering on what you promise and getting relationships to a mutual trust level. I can literally go years without seeing someone and when we meet again the relationship we have built makes it look like we have been networking together nonstop, so build those relationships by being a giving person and those relationships will form.

Be clear on your target Market

You are not sure what to talk about and who to talk to, what is your target market?

This is one of the most crucial things about networking and one area where I was very poor at for too long a period. I am now at the stage where I am happy to train people in networking skills having been doing it 10 years but mainly because I made lots of mistakes and I am now aware of them.

The biggest area was in not defining my target market, so although I made relationship easily and was as giving as I could be, I confused people!! I had a reputation for being a good bloke, always happy to help out and signpost, as well as always getting back to people when I promised. I was polite I listened and generally had a great reputation, so what was wrong?

Clarity is key

The big problem was that I was not telling people what I wanted from them, despite the fact many of them wanted to help me. The reason was I was not consistent with what I brought to the meetings.

The reason for this was I was out of work and looking for opportunities but whilst I did that I met networkers who were happy to have me as a commissioned associate, so I became muddled with my offering.

I look back now and laugh at it, but it was wasted time, I needed to have stuck with one thing and then I would have been clear to what I was looking for and people would have known if they could have helped or not.

Help others

Once I learned the lesson things got better and I started helping newbies by making them aware of the mistake. Many when asked what their target market was would say somebody or anybody who.... This is not targeted, and I would reply that I have networked extensively but never come across Mr or Mrs Somebody or anybody!!

I would quickly follow this up by pointing out that I and people like me had large networks and therefore needed a more specific target like a senior partner is a professional service company in Reading, then I could signpost them to 2 or 3 options.

The other way of concentrating their mind was by miming that I had just brought to the meeting their number 1 target and asked them to tell me who it is.

In Summary:

So, be specific about the person or companies who are in your target market and see how your networking results improve.

Networking is good but!

Following on from last series of Networking blogs I want to raise your awareness of what to do after you have networked so that you start cementing that relationship and not let it drift as many do.

What to do after your first event

So, you have returned after your first network meeting and feel a mixture of relief and positivity. You have done your best to follow my tips to the best of your ability and you certainly collected some business cards.

Follow up

Your need to sort out a to do list from what you have gathered from the event. This may simply be adding details into your CRM, but hopefully you will have a few things to do to help those you met.

It is imperative that you do these actions as this is what you will be judged on, there is nothing worse than someone saying they will do something then just not following up. Remember networking is not about selling but about building relationships, treat others how you wish to be treated. You will learn that some people are just in the room for themselves and just take, rarely give. Look to have conversations with people who want to help. This of course is easier said than done, and you will learn who to avoid and who the influencers are. In the meantime, have that get out of jail card ready, even if it is that you must go to the cloakroom.

Carry on the conversation

So, once you have found the right people after the inevitable hit and miss, you need to continue building the conversation and therefore the relationship. One way is to commit to going regularly to the group where you met them, as face to face is the best method to forming a good relationship. Two things though work against this and that is the time between meetings is usually a month and that there will be some sort of financial commitment involved.

My suggestion is that most groups use a 2-guest visit system as a try before you buy, so go to as many groups as you can, so you can see if the "room" suits you. Even different venues for the same overall networking group can have very big differences.

Now this takes time and money, so you need to allow for this in any marketing budget but be aware it is often months before you become trusted, which is quite natural. One thing that you can do to help build these relationships is to take them online and use social media.

Facebook often has groups that correspond to the physical ones so that will be useful, I personally use LinkedIn for most of my online networking and it is possibly more important that physical networking in building relationships due to its 24/7/365 nature.

In Summary:

The follow up is very important but so is keeping in touch. I use LinkedIn as it is the primary Business social media tool. How to use it, well I have a series of blogs on LinkedIn to get you started.

Active listening

You attend a networking event and are not satisfied with how it went. All the conversations you had and cards you collected just seem to be a blur in your memory.

To listen is to win

Don't worry it happens at the beginning as very few people are taught how to network effectively. So, what can you do different to change this around?

There is one area a lot of people do not understand and therefore don't apply and that is active listening. Active listening is when you actually listen to what the other person is saying rather than thinking of what you are going to say or generally not being active in the conversation.

People favourite subject is normally themselves, but to grow an effective relationship and add to your network, they also need to listen. There will be little bits of information within what they are saying which will give you clues on how to direct the conversation. Now we all know that the best relationships are where both sides win, but it depends if they are working a long or short game.

What I mean by this is are they looking to build relationships or after a quick sale and move on. By using active listening, you should pick up some clues from what they say, but don't worry, this tales a bit of time.

If by active listening you feel that you are just listening to a sales pitch then use a get out tactic, as they may pretend to be interested in you but are not really, or they are the worst type who don't care and show it and still don't care because they are in it for number 1 only.

Making use of the room

If you are lucky and get talking to a seasoned networker (good tip is to ask to be introduced to 1 by your hosts) they will take the time to listen to you and offer help, as it is in all good networker's interests to have a bigger network.

Some people when you actively listen to their story do not seem to be an obvious fit, but show signs of interest in what you have to say. These can become your advocates and point people in your direction, whilst you feel you will be happy to do the same for them.

One section of the networking set are professional service people and often people will think of them as dull and of no use, and yes some certainly are, but the better ones are a reliable source, because who are their clients?? I am sure in there are companies that fall into your target demographic.

In Summary:

So, go with a plan, know your target and listen, you will be amazed at what you pick up on that you would normally miss whilst preparing a response.

I have started networking what next

You have been to a varied selection of networking groups and met a lot of new people and you have followed some of the hints and tips from my blog, so what next.

Relationship Building

It is a well-known fact that people buy from people, they buy from people they like and trust, people that are like themselves. The best way to get trust is by building a strong relationship with a person. The best way is always face to face, but this is not always possible so schedule call, skype call or similar.

Follow up

It is essential that if you have offered to do something for someone that you follow up in a timely fashion. You need to do this when your meeting is fresh in the other person's

Contact

There are numerous ways to connect with people following meeting them at an event, and their business card should be a useful source of information. I personally use LinkedIn as my preferred platform, but many use Facebook, so see which arena they use and send a connection request, but make it personal to remind them about you and where you met.

So, you have now networked and met a few people and started a few conversations and hopefully promised to do something for the people you met, what next. Well you will be forming an idea of which groups are going to help you with your target market. This will be direct with the group members or through their network, and from this you will see how often you need to attend. You will find that you will become more selective after a while but do allow time and money to do a lot when you first start.

I have started networking what next- Part two

You have been to a varied selection of networking groups and met a lot of new people and you have started following up on the promises that you made, so what next.

Keep Building

You are now working on you network plan and attending events accordingly, where you meet people you have had conversations with before as well as started new ones. I see there being 3 stages to relationships, start, build and Maintain. You will find that this structure you fall into naturally both at events and online.

It is similar to a sales funnel in that you need to keep adding new people in at the top and then try and get as many people out the bottom, but unlike a sales funnel there are multiple outlets!!

Multiple outlets

You may never actually do business with the people in the room but still get value from the room. This is because as you grow those relationships trust starts to form, and especially if you have done something for someone. Now if trust is built then they will happily turn into what is often called your unpaid salesforce. The reason for this is that they are happy to signpost people to you. Now many people call this a referral as well, I personally think that I signpost people and usually give them a couple of options. The reason I do this is that unless I have paid them money to do something for me I am not able to refer them, but I am in a position to signpost people to them as I feel confident from the relationship that has been built. Also, when you refer you are also putting your reputation on the line.

Also, you may find synergy with some people and be able to work together as a joint venture or just by adding each other's offerings to your product basket.So, there are 3 main positive outputs from the networking, people signposting others to you, working with someone at a certain level or selling your goods and services. All these are likely to start face to face but move online as it is quicker and easier.

Bonus Blog

What type of event should I go to?

I am often asked this, and I can honestly say that you should try as many as you can, even from the same organisation, as I have found they can differ a lot dependent on location. Also, you need to consider the target market and where they are likely to network.

A lot of the groups are aimed at smaller companies or find themselves in that area, as a lot of micro businesses go networking. Micro businesses make up over 90% of all registered companies in the UK, so it is not hard to see why you find so many at networking events. They are mainly there to get their name out there, but also for the community feel that groups give them. It is a lonely world for a start-up, often being just 1 or 2 people, so the opportunity to be in a business arena is a fantastic way of belonging to something bigger.

Somewhere in their plan (if they have one!) is to meet with larger companies as they will fall in their target market. The trouble is that they have a slightly different approach and quite often are told to go networking rather than it be their own choice.

As the attendee is likely to be claiming back the costs on their expenses their drive is different. They are also likely to be SME's and professional service company's local office, so they are there to promote their name in a room with potentially many similar companies.

There are some groups that will allow only 1 company from one industry, but the downside I find to these referrals based groups is that if you don't click with a certain company there is no one else in that group that covers that speciality.

If you have a clear idea of your target, a visit to as many separate groups and venues will show you which rooms you should be in. Being in the wrong room can be a comfortable arena but is a waste of time and money if your targets don't attend. Your best bet here is to build relationships and rely on them referring you to someone in your target market.

This does happen, but it takes time so why not spend some time networking where your target market does. This may often mean a bigger investment for you, but will give you the chance to be in the right room.

So, my advice is plan, budget then attend as many as you can and once you have, then work out how often you need to attend certain groups, if at all, and identify others that you need to be at but throw up more of a challenge financially and access wise. The rewards could be worth the outlay, but you won't know to you try as it's all about the quality of the room.

These blogs were just little stories with hints and tips based on my experience and I hope that you found them useful as a learning or affirmation tool.

CHAPTER THIRTEEN

TIPS I HAVE USED, AND I TRUST

This next section is a collection of tips that I learned from my networking and that I apply still to this day. At an event, I always aim to arrive earlier than the advertised time. The reason I do this is so that I can get a chance to speak to the organisers and even help if required. It also means I get a parking place as sometimes these are limited. The next thing is the reception desk and in my experience, these can vary greatly in quality.

From the Chamber with nice printed plastic badges and neat guest lists at the top, down to a typed list for the hosts to tick off attendees and your name hand written on a paper label. Some events that are more social do away with this completely.

As a gentleman, I am likely to be wearing a jacket and the obvious place to put your badge is on your left breast pocket. I suggest that is not the best place for your badge because of something I was taught very early on. That is when you go to shake hands with someone your right hand comes around in front of you, and as it does your torso twists. This makes your left side, and badge move away from the person making it harder for them to read. If it is on the right side, it twists into view making it easier for the person to read it and confirm that they have heard your name correctly.

> **WEAR YOUR NAME BADGE ON YOUR RIGHT HAND SIDE**

Another upside to this is if you tell people why you wear it on the right they often take this suggestion up and remember you more because of it. I also believe that in certain cultures the movement away of the badge can be deemed as being rude as you are taking it away from their eyesight. The other tip on badges is that I would strongly recommend a magnetic one as this is easier to wear, does not mark your clothing and is consistent. Much preferable to a handwritten sticky label I am sure you will agree. There will be sometimes you are asked to just wear the badge you are given but these are rare and having your own badge becomes part of you and your branding. These are a worthwhile investment and don't cost the earth.

I mentioned Branding there and this I find as quite important, especially for the owner managers. It is less so with the corporates as they will follow the company line, but as an individual you have license to create your own branding and this helps you be more memorable.

One of my network has a lime green Mercedes and always wears a jacket to match. Another always wore a pink tie and a close friend of mine always wears a 3-piece suit and a pink tie. He also carries the colour throughout his marketing material.

> BE CONSISTENT WITH YOUR BRANDING BUT PLEASE DO HAVE SOME BRANDING

My habit of arriving early also gives me the chance to scope out the layout which. This comes from my years of running events, but comes in handy to know where everything is. Even this little bit of knowledge when shared with others raises people's opinion of you, and that can never be a bad thing.

If there is a guest list I will cast an eye over it to see if anyone matching my target type is booked on. If so I will station myself near the registration desk, so I can see them come in. Sometimes I will have found them on LinkedIn and have an idea of what they look like but sometimes not, so being within earshot is beneficial to me. I don't normally pounce straight away as I would prefer they settle in first.

If on the other hand it is obvious by whom they are, that they will be constantly engaged in discussion I will take the opportunity to get in first.

TRY AND ASK THE FIRST QUESTION

In fact, it is one of my top tips at a networking event, get in first. Asking the first question is a great tactic to see if the person in front of you is someone you want to be talking to, and for how long for. If you ask them what they do or what brought them to the event you can get a feel for what they are like.

This is not perfect but the "me" centric people reveal themselves very quickly. Listen carefully to what they say and when they ask you in turn what you do, take the appropriate words to reply with.

What I mean by this is if they seem like someone who could be good to connect with then tell them what you do, the problems you solve and what you are looking for. This gives them a clear picture of how they might be able to help you, and of course you too may come up with things that may help them. This is the start of the relationship and how you follow up can determine how strong this becomes.If on the other hand you feel you need to get out of the conversation, then there are several ways to do this.

Some basic ones such as the need to go to the toilet to a very polite but firm "we are both here to network and meet new people so let's go network" or something similar, which in their minds is a positive. Other times you may need to be more creative, such as pretend to hear your phone vibrate and claim it is an important call. Or you could say that you spotted someone you are desperate to catch up with. Most people will not be offended

by this and will let you out, maybe with a card exchange before you go. Again, offer to take their card and move on. My favourite and cheeky one, and to be honest not at all professional, was a pre-arranged one. This only works when you have built up a network, not in the early days.
I would agree with a person in my network that we would be the others "out".

This way we could get out of the current conversation and be welcomed by the other regardless. My twist was the partner in this was an elegant beautiful blond lady called Emily, who, when I spotted I would tell the other parson that I needed to go hug that lovely blonde over there. Most people having seen her would immediately let me go thinking that it would not happen, but of course a big hug and double cheek kiss, and a quick catch up chat was the pre-arranged outcome.

> ### Have some good reasons that you can move on from a conversation

Now that was an effortless way to start a conversation with a person as it was prearranged, but what about a full room, where can you start?

There will be various configuration of people talking in groups at events and this is what I remember being taught by Mark Pearl, and has helped me over the years.

Let us start with 2 people in a conversation as this seems the easiest to enter but it can be the hardest and one you should not try to. The giveaway sign is that they will be standing square on feet facing each other and holding eye contact.

They are in a deep conversation and would not welcome an interruption, so be polite and leave them to it. If on the other hand their stance is open, not head on but at a slight angle to each other, and are freely gazing around, then you can approach. The open stance is an open invitation to join them, so take the opportunity if you want. Also, if one is open and the other person stance is closed, then the person who has an open stance, is looking for an out. So, if you are feeling brave you can join in, you also may well find yourself doing the same thing.

A group of 3 is a bit harder to gauge as be default they are in a triangle but you can still see when its open as a gap usually naturally appears. In both the open 2 & 3 groups it is always polite to ask to join them and once you get the nod introduce yourself, and then try getting in that first question. Let us go back from a group of 3 to a single person. This is not a group, but you will see people standing on their own at events. Some will be in planning mode, if it is that then like me they are probably trying to get a sneaky coffee and bacon bap in, whilst working on their next few moves.

This brings up another tip, you cannot gracefully network with a cup in one hand and food in the other. So, go to the side, sit down if seating is available or take this time to have a chat to a friend. This should matter's less that you are engaging in a conversation whilst consuming food whilst you listen.

When you see a person on their own, it is quite possible, like you were once, or possibly still are, not ensure what best to do in this situation. It is often quoted that one of the most stressful things you can do is public speaking, but networking with strangers is not far off it. Luckily both become easier with practice, so the more you practice the better you will get.

The person standing on their own is likely to be relieved if you approach them in a friendly way. They will appreciate that you have made the effort. This is because unless they are properly trained, or have read this book or the supporting website, they may not be that polished. So, take the opportunity to help them feel more comfortable about the situation.

I still have people remind me that I was the first person they met and how I made them at ease and helped them, and that can be as long as 8 years ago. Yes, helping people is a very positive thing to do when trying to build a relationship. So, spend some time with them giving them some idea of what to expect, point out KPI's if you know them, and introduce them to a group so that they can start or continue their journey. If it was your first event, then would it not be great to get that help?

Now let us look at groups of 4 or more which usually form at an event. There is normally at least one and it will have its leader who is orchestrating things, so they are the best person to catch the eye of to join in.

Better still if you spot someone that you know then catch their eye and they will give you an in and are very likely to introduce you. To judge the conversations at a network meeting, you can either study basic body language, read a book or use natural intuition, any of these will help you to make an excellent choice.

They will help you read a room, and also see how engaged people you are talking to. It still amazes me that a lot of people just read body language really poorly, from very obvious signals.

These can be, loss of eye contact, glances at watch or phone, and a lack of real conversation. On the other hand, if you spot others doing it to you then take the hint and close out the conversation.

> STUDY GROUPS AT AN EVENT AND CHOSE
> THE OPEN ONES TO JOIN

TIPS I HAVE USED, AND I TRUST

You are looking for rapport, which can be taught, but I strongly believe it is in all of us, just some believe more than others. Trust me when I say that it is in your locker, it might just be at the back, covered up.

In Rapport like many other things you can go through the classic 4 stages of competence as provided by Maslow.

Unconscious incompetence	Unaware you are doing it wrong
Conscious Incompetence	Aware you are doing it wrong
Conscious competence	Aware you are doing it right
Unconscious competence	Unware you are doing it right
	Aware you are doing it right

The last state is where you want to get, and it takes a lot of practice, but is well worth it. I often catch myself in the unconscious competence mode which its self is a level above, as you are automatically doing it right without thought. Here my subconscious has given me a little jolt, and it is like an outer body experience looking down at yourself. You catch yourself doing it right.

So, you are in a conversation and you have asked the first question, so use active listening. I know this is hard early on as you are running through what you are going to say in your head. Active listening has 2 main advantages, and they are that the other person will see that you are interested as your body language will tell them.

Secondly you will hear things that you can pick up on when it is your turn to talk. This will allow for a better conversation and the more likelihood of business cards being swapped.

Your body language is a great communicator, so as well as picking up on signals that the person you are talking to gives off, they too are picking up signals that you are giving off. A lot of business and self-help books mention a study that gives you a percentage of how we communicate. Here is a typical explanation. They quote

Professor Mehrabian who combined the statistical results of two studies and came up with the now famous rule. That is that communication is only 7percent verbal and 93 percent non-verbal. The non-verbal component was made up of body language (55 percent) and tone of voice (38 percent). Although this is often quoted it only applied to a certain study and even the good professor is quoted as saying that it is not a general rule. Having said that it does show a good representation of the split in gereral and how important the components are.

> STUDY GROUPS AT AN EVENT AND CHOSE THE OPEN ONES TO JOIN

CHAPTER FOURTEEN

KEEP ON TRACK

Now don't forget when you are engaged in conversation at an event that you have a plan. This will mean that you need to speak to a certain number of people during the event. Now if you are really clear on your target then the people you are in conversation with will be more likely to point you in the direction of someone in the room. They would have listened to you talk about your target and point you at a person they think will fit the bill They could also say that they know someone in their network who would be worth getting in touch with.

KPI's get to the stage where people are advised to talk to them, so they do not need to go in search of a conversation if they don't want to. Most will of course because they will have a plan. I found myself at the stage, that if people wanted to know about local networking or the chamber, then people where pointed in my direction. This is what you are looking for, that unpaid sales force of people who will automatically point people in your direction as the go to expert, whether you are in the room or not.

Being the go to expert is what you really should aim for, so when someone says they are looking for an expert in your field, your network automatically thinks of you. You get to be in this position by continually giving, helping and following up. This builds you a reputation of reliability and knowledge which is a priceless asset.

It takes a while to build up to this stage and you must be consistent because it can take moments to lose your good reputation. So, if you say that you are going to do something, then make sure you darn well go and do it. If you cannot get back to the person in the timescale that you gave then let them know, do not leave them hanging, waiting for you.

FOLLOW UP OR GET FORGOTTEN

I really cannot emphasise enough that the follow up is a really large part of the relationship building, it should be automatic in any business, but rarely is.

I see that there are mainly 4 parts to the relationship, those being firstly building rapport, then building trust, signposting and finally referring. You could say that there is another level and that is a partnership, joint venture or collaboration. I love the idea of collaboration so much that I formed a LinkedIn group which attracted a reasonable number of local business owners. Once it built momentum,

I then took it offline and held two events. At these events I taught them what collaboration is all about and the power it had in business. I also told them anyone referring to the selling word early on could leave there and then, as they have misunderstood the point of these events. I split them up gave them tasks, and I am proud to say more than one collaboration project was born from these events.

They basically looked at things from a different angle and found ways to include companies where they had not seen an obvious alignment previously. This happened in my year out of work, and I strongly believe looking back at these events that had I not found work, then these groups would have got well established. Unfortunately, when I could no longer run the events or the Linkedin group no one took up the reigns.

The LinkedIn groups exists still, and I have plans to shake them back to life when I leave employment and find myself with more time. I will then use them to give back to the online community what I have learned, like the motivation for writing this book.

The setting up and running of LinkedIn groups is also a good move when you are networking as it shows that you are willing to help and also to take responsibility. It will also demonstrate that you exhibit management and leadership skills, which can only hold you in good stead. Also, in my case it showed consistency as I was also involved in physically helping to run networking groups.

By helping to run two regular monthly groups it elevated my standing in the networking community. It showed I was willing to get involved and stand up and be counted. It also showed that I was also willing to help the groups and the overall business. I became relied upon to step into groups and help when the ambassadors could not make it. I also helped set up groups across the area as the company expanded. I still communicate with the owners to this day as I think that the model they used for their groups really helped micro businesses.

Because of this win/win relationship I met with them and we discussed a full-time role within the organisation which would involve setting up groups across the country as the company expanded from its Thames Valley base. The reason I believe that they wanted to talk to me was that I understood what worked and what didn't, and was very good at choosing venues for the groups.

If you decide to run an event for yourself or for others, then there are some basic things to look for. How easy is the venue to get to, is there adequate parking, free being preferred? Is the room easy to get to, is it a decent size and finally how keen the venue is to form a relationship with you? Tick these boxes and you are choosing a potentially good venue.

I say potentially as you will only really know how the venue see you and your group after the first few events. It still amazes me the number of venues that did not send along staff to mingle and promote the venue to these business people. Also, those venues, that after the honeymoon period seemed to lose all interest and the service levels dropped right off. Get engagement from the venue and it will help you and the group no end, see it dropping off and then you need to talk with them to find out why.

Now back to the subject of following up, again I will state this is the most important part and if not done properly it can undo all the excellent work that proceeded it. Why would you go into a room full of mainly strangers, start some conversations, get some cards, promise to do a follow up (even as simple as connecting on LinkedIn) and then simply not deliver?

But I see it happen time and time again, that is why I say go with a plan and do not be a card collector. Quality over quantity is what works, and it also allows you to follow up with true intent and meaning. I mean are you really going to follow up all 25 cards that you collected in a timely manner? If you do, then very well done.

But I would ask you to look at your time management. Also, how many relationships can you start at the same time? In the early days as you are building It may be tempting to collect all these cards and start all these relationships, and if you do then please do not over promise.

> ONLY TAKE A BUSINESS CARD IF YOU ARE ACTUALLY GOING TO FOLLOW UP, DON'T BE A COLLECTOR

Networking is often the start of a new relationship which may turn into new business for you. Networking is the face to face side of starting and building strong relationships with people, you need to invest in it on a regular basis and you should put aside some money in your marketing budget for it.

In the early days you will need to invest more time in attending events than you do as your business grows, and yes, I strongly believe that face to face interactions to be the best. What I hope will happen for you is that you get busy delivering paid work to your clients, and therefore have less time for networking. What I must say is that you must not stop networking, you need to be seen and be in peoples consciousnesses.

When you get to this stage it is even more important that you turn to LinkedIn or Facebook, dependent on where your prospect reside.

You need to allocate time rather than money here, but you do need to do this. I will demonstrate in my next book how you can use LinkedIn to your advantage, for both building and maintaining your connections, or as Seth Godin called them, your tribe.

CHAPTER FIFTEEN

The Networking Conversion System

This book and its follow up about how I used LinkedIn have been vital components in me setting up a business to bring my experience to people. I had the contents of these books and all that experience but how to bring it into reality? The answer sits in the pages of this book and that is my network. I had been paying into the bank of Network for 10 years now was the time to make withdrawals.

The response from my network blew me away and the 9 months prior to launching my company was filled with advice and help from not only my direct network, but theirs as well. I was signposted to new people and they have become part of my network and have been brilliant with the help they have given me. I identified my target markets and narrowed down what I was going to offer, which was the hardest part for me and I am sure for a lot of people starting out. I eventually removed various elements, so I was clear on what I was offering and who to. I created a website with a lot of help from a lovely lady and got Business cards printed, so I thought I was ready but, oh no there still seemed something missing despite when telling people I knew, they go it.

So back to my network and someone I admire, Richard Woods (yes him off the Apprentice). I had joined his Academy and part of this was a 1-2-1 meeting to see where he could help your business. Well this meeting put in place the last piece and that was the delivery of my knowledge and experience through a system. So the Networking Conversion System was born and I went back to my creative network to get the central Infographic created, and added it to all my collateral.

The system takes you from planning to the pitch meeting, therefore showing people how to turn networking from a cost to a lead generator and then into the sales arena and potential revenue. More details can be found on my website www.solidsilversolutions.co.uk

I do hope that you found this book informative and an easy read as my aim is to give people a resource to help them improve their skills and build a strong network.

ACKNOWLEDGEMENTS

Warren Cass	For throwing down the challenge of writing a book.
Mark Perl	For giving his time free to educate and train me in the correct use of LinkedIn.
Sue Reeves	For allowing me to get involved in her network.
Jim Ewan	For the training on presentation skills.
Brian Murphy	For all the help via the executive Job Club.
Richard Woods	For taking me under his wing and helping with getting these books to print and devising my delivery system
Anthony Stears	Half my age but an inspiration and mentor on my journey to solopreneurship.
Claire Boyles	For spending her precious time getting a slick website into shape and helping with marketing..
Kes Williams	A wonderful friend and Graphic designer who worked on the books layout and images as well as some of those on my website and marketing material.
Finally:	the literally thousands of people I have met on my journey and those that are still with me on the next phase, for without this network I could not have got to where I am now, I thank you all.

www.ingramcontent.com/pod-product-compliance
Lightning Source LLC
Chambersburg PA
CBHW070111230526
45472CB00004B/1218